THAT'S SO WEIRD!

KATHLEEN LONG BOSTROM

Worthy kids
ideals®

ISBN-13: 978-1-945470-28-8

Published by WorthyKids/Ideals, an imprint of Worthy Publishing Group, a division of Worthy Media, Inc., in association with Museum of the Bible.

museum of the Bible
BOOKS

Copyright © 2017 by Museum of the Bible Books
409 3rd St. SW
Washington, D.C. 20024-4706
Museum of the Bible is an innovative, global, educational institution whose purpose is to invite all people to engage with the history, narrative, and impact of the Bible.

Library of Congress CIP data is on file

Unless otherwise indicated, scripture quotations are from the ESV® Bible (The Holy Bible, English Standard Version®), copyright © 2001 by Crossway, a publishing ministry of Good News Publishers. Used by permission. All rights reserved.

Cover design by Eve DeGrie
Produced with the assistance of Hudson Bible (www.HudsonBible.com)
Illustrations by Aliaksei Zhuro

Printed and bound in the U.S.A.
RRD-Craw_Aug17_1

DID YOU KNOW?

Did you know that the Bible tells about one king who had couches made of gold and silver? Or that the oldest man mentioned in the Bible lived to be 969 years old? Do you know which prophet in the Bible could run faster than a horse?

The Bible tells many interesting and important stories, but it also has lots of fun and fascinating facts that you might not expect. *That's So Weird!* collects more than 100 of these bits of Bible trivia and tells you where in the Bible (book, chapter, and verse) you can find them. We used the Protestant edition of the Bible, which has 66 books in the Old and New Testaments.

Whether you want to learn more about some of your favorite Bible stories or want to discover some of the amazing and interesting—and downright weird—facts presented in the Bible, we think you'll enjoy what you see here.

Ready to learn something new? Turn the page. Jump in!

People say **money doesn't grow on trees,** but did you know money was once found inside a fish? Jesus told Peter to pay his taxes by catching a fish and then pulling a coin out of its mouth!

(Matthew 17:26–27)

APPLE? ORANGE? POMEGRANATE?

Nobody knows for sure what type of fruit Adam and Eve ate in the garden of Eden. (Genesis 3:6)

WHAT'S

6+6+6+6?

One man in the Bible, descended from the giants, could solve that on his finger and toes.

He had **6 fingers** on each hand and **6 toes** on each foot.

(2 Samuel 21:20)

The Bible mentions
three sets of twins.

When Isaac and Rebekah's twin sons, Jacob and Esau, were born, Esau came first and Jacob was holding on to his heel!

(Genesis 25:24–26, 38:27; John 11:16)

The Dead Sea, mentioned in the Bible, **is actually a lake.** It is nearly **10 TIMES** saltier than the ocean.

(Joshua 15:5)

GOD told **ABRAHAM** he would have as many CHILDREN, GRANDCHILDREN, AND GREAT-GRANDCHILDREN as there are **STARS in the SKY—** far too many to count!

(Genesis 15:5, 17:5)

GOLIATH

WAS TALL, POSSIBLY OVER **9** **FEET TALL!**

That's TALLER than the inside of an elevator, **so he would need to TAKE THE STAIRS!**

(1 Samuel 17:4)

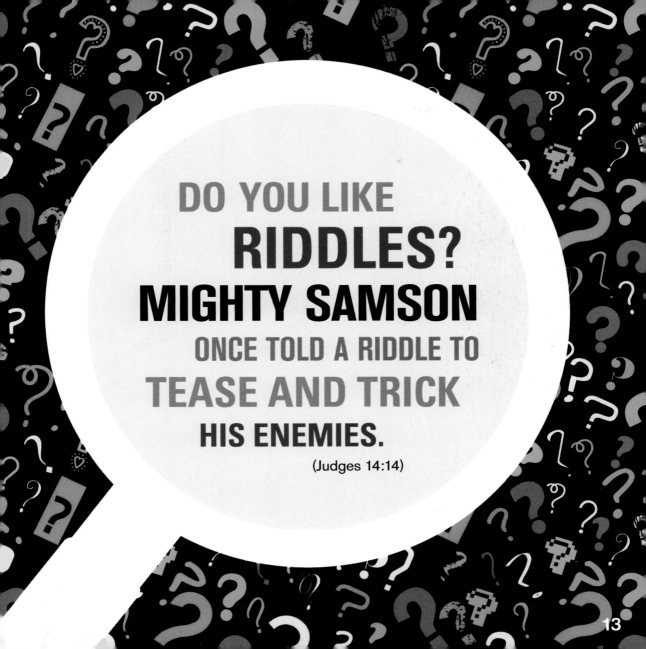

DO YOU LIKE **RIDDLES?** **MIGHTY SAMSON** ONCE TOLD A RIDDLE TO **TEASE AND TRICK** HIS ENEMIES.

(Judges 14:14)

A female gnat can lay

300

eggs in one day,

and they grow
into adults in only

one week.

Gnats bite people and
animals, and it's painful.

**They can destroy
plants, too, so the
plague of gnats
in Egypt would
have been terrible!**

(Exodus 8:16–17)

LEPROSY

In the Bible, people who had **leprosy**, a terrible skin disease, **were sent away** to live in groups by themselves. Today, leprosy can be treated— **and even cured.**

(Leviticus 13:1–3, 45–46; Luke 17:12)

SHEEP

are mentioned in the Bible more than any other animal—

over **350 times.**

(Psalm 78:52)

BAA!

ABSALOM,

A HANDSOME PRINCE IN THE BIBLE,
CUT HIS LONG HAIR ONLY ONCE A YEAR.

The trimmings weighed about 5 POUNDS – as much as a bag of SUGAR.

(2 Samuel 14:26)

There
are about **25**
MUSICAL
INSTRUMENTS
mentioned in the Bible—
including the **TRUMPET,**
HARP, LYRE, FLUTE,
and **CYMBALS.**

(Exodus 19:16; Psalm 150:3–6;
Daniel 3:5–15)

KING OG'S BED

was **6 feet wide** and about **14 feet long** — big enough to fit **AN ELEPHANT** (at least a skinny one).

(Deuteronomy 3:11)

GOLIATH'S armor weighed about **125** pounds, as much as a full-grown **Great Dane.**

(1 Samuel 17:5–6)

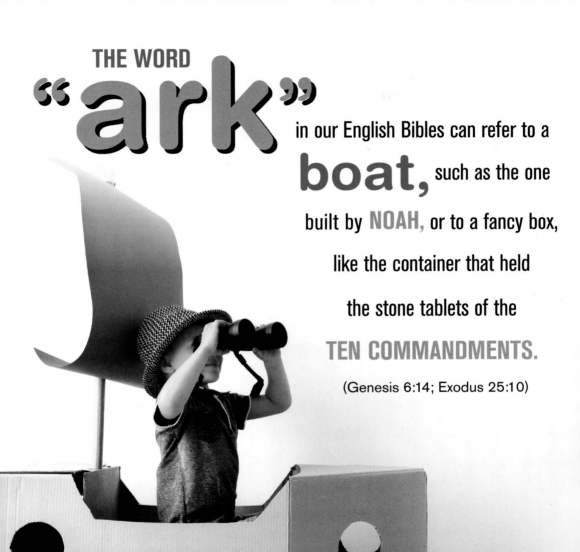

THE WORD "ark" in our English Bibles can refer to a **boat,** such as the one built by **NOAH,** or to a fancy box, like the container that held the stone tablets of the **TEN COMMANDMENTS.**

(Genesis 6:14; Exodus 25:10)

NOAH'S ARK was taller than a **three-story building** and longer than a **football field,** yet it had **ONLY ONE** DOOR.

(Genesis 6:15–16)

I wish there were an elevator.

King Ahasuerus
threw a party
that lasted for

SIX
MONTHS.

(Esther 1:3–5)

PARTY ON!

23

Angels told Lot

and his wife to run away so they
wouldn't be destroyed along with their city.
"Hurry!" the angels said. **"Don't look back!"**
When Lot's wife ignored this advice, she became a
pillar of **salt.**
(Genesis 19:15, 17, 26)

LOT'S WIFE

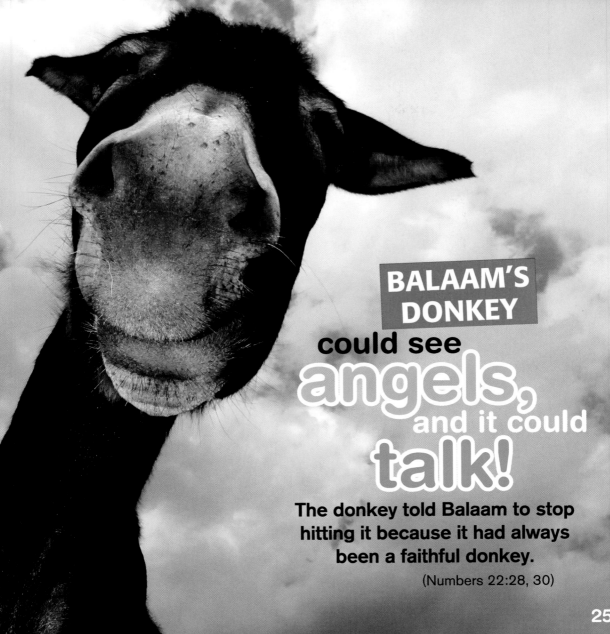

BALAAM'S DONKEY

could see

angels,

and it could

talk!

The donkey told Balaam to stop
hitting it because it had always
been a faithful donkey.

(Numbers 22:28, 30)

GOD placed a **rainbow** in the sky as a **promise** that a **flood** would never again destroy the earth.

(Genesis 9:14–16)

Some rainbows
are a full circle.
The bottom half is
hidden by the earth
and can only be
seen from above.

The Israelites **wandered** in the desert
for 40 years,
but their clothes and sandals **never wore out.**

(Deuteronomy 29:5)

Moses's mother

hid him in a basket made of **papyrus**, a plant found along the **Nile River**. Papyrus was also used to make rope, mats, sandals, perfume, food, clothes, and paper.

(Exodus 2:3)

Our word **"paper"** comes from the word "papyrus."

A SERIOUS HAILSTORM

can cause a lot of **DAMAGE,**
even **DEATH.** Hailstones have been measured as large as
a softball and weighing two pounds! When the plague of hail struck
Egypt, **GOD WARNED THE ISRAELITES**
to get themselves and their animals to safety so they wouldn't be killed.

(Exodus 9:18–19, 25)

ACCORDING TO THE BOOK OF

PROVERBS,

SOME OF THE WISEST CREATURES ARE

ANTS,

HYRAXES,

LOCUSTS,
&
LIZARDS.

(Proverbs 30:24–28)

**WHAT IS
A HYRAX?**

A HYRAX IS A
ROCK BADGER.

Many **mountains** are mentioned in the **Bible.**

Some mountains are **UNDERWATER,** including the longest mountain range in the world, which is on the bottom of the **ATLANTIC OCEAN.**

(Psalm 46:2)

Joseph could **predict the future** with his **dreams.** This got him into trouble with his brothers, but it also HELPED HIM GET OUT OF JAIL when **Pharaoh** needed someone to interpret his dreams.

(Genesis 37:5–11, 41:15–40)

WHERE DID

Adam and Eve

get **CLOTHES** to wear?

God made clothes of animal skins.

(Genesis 3:21)

The first color mentioned in the BIBLE is **green**, used to describe the type of plants that God created for FOOD.

(Genesis 1:30)

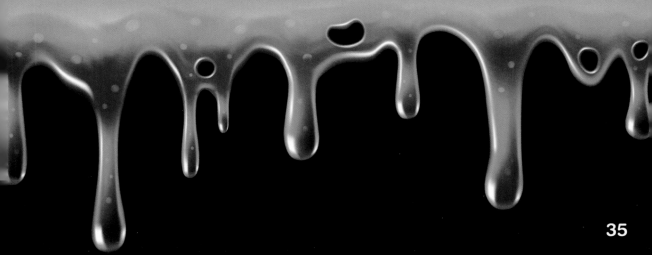

FLUTES (PIPES) and **STRINGED INSTRUMENTS** (SUCH AS HARPS) are early **MUSICAL INSTRUMENTS** named in the Bible. Pianos weren't invented **UNTIL NEARLY 1700!**

(Genesis 4:21)

SAMSON scooped some **HONEY** out of the carcass of a dead lion and ate it!

Then he gave some to his parents, and they ate it too!

GROSS!

(Judges 14:8–9)

3

PEOPLE

in the English Bible
have a name that
begins with F:

FELIX, FESTUS, and FORTUNATUS.

(Acts 23:24;25:1;
1 Corinthians 16:17)

The Israelites **melted their earrings** to make a **statue** of a **golden calf.**

(Exodus 32:2–4)

We don't know what kind of fish **SWALLOWED JONAH,** but it must have had

huge jaws!

The **whale shark** is the largest known fish today. A male whale shark can weigh over **20 tons,** about the same as **3 elephants.**

NOW THAT'S A BIG FISH!

(Jonah 1:17)

BRR! The Bible mentions only one **SNOWY DAY,** although **SNOW** is mentioned several times to describe the color **WHITE.**

(2 Samuel 23:20; Matthew 28:3)

Cheese is mentioned only three times in the Bible.

SO MUCH FOR PIZZA!

(1 Samuel 17:18; 2 Samuel 17:29; Job 10:10)

King Solomon had **4,000** stalls for horses and chariots, plus **12,000** horsemen.

(2 Chronicles 9:25)

Those must have been some really big stables!

A **boy** shared his lunch and **Jesus** used it to feed over **5,000** people.

(John 6:9)

KING
NEBUCHADNEZZAR
made a **GOLD STATUE** of himself that was about **90** feet high— or almost as tall as a nine-story building.

(Daniel 3:1)

The **ISRAELITES**

DESTROYED A TEMPLE

of the

FALSE GOD, BAAL.

Then they turned it into a

BATHROOM!

(2 Kings 10:26–27)

How did you spend your spring break?

Zimri was **king of Israel —**

for only one week.

(1 Kings 16:15)

TWELVE BOOKS of the **Bible** begin with the letter

J.

How many can you name **without peeking?**

JAMES

Job

JOHN

Joel

Jeremiah

1 JOHN

2 JOHN

3 JOHN

JUDE

Jonah

JUDGES

Joshua

SERAPHIM,

the angels mentioned in the book of Isaiah, had

6 wings!

(Isaiah 6:2)

DANIEL and his friends **REFUSED** the food and wine that **KING NEBUCHADNEZZAR** wanted them to eat. They ate **VEGETABLES** and drank **WATER** instead. Theirs was a healthy eating choice!

(Daniel 1:15)

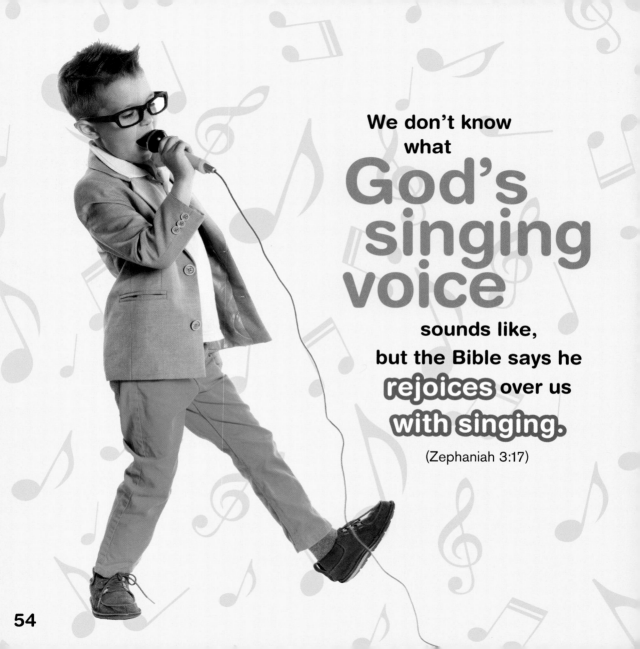

We don't know what **God's singing voice** sounds like, but the Bible says he **rejoices** over us **with singing.**

(Zephaniah 3:17)

WHO IS THE MOST FEARSOME OF THE BEASTS? According to **Job**, it is **LEVIATHAN,** a sea creature with **terrifying teeth** who **sneezes smoke** and **spits fire.** (Job 41)

Leviathan

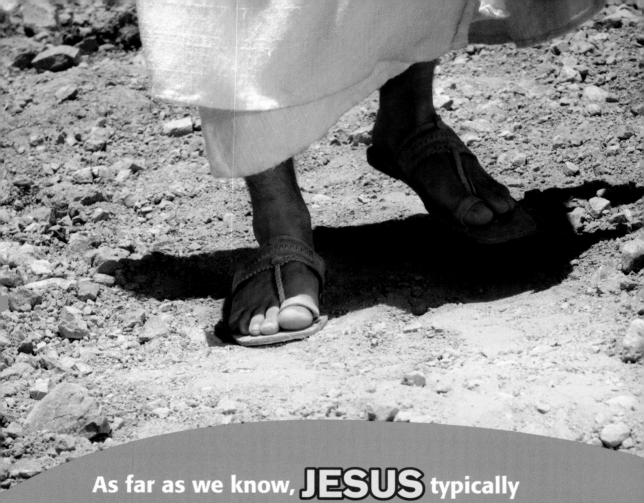

As far as we know, **JESUS** typically traveled on **FOOT** or by **BOAT.** One time he **RODE A DONKEY.**

(Mark 11:7)

KING DAVID

was a **talented musician** and a **great dancer**, although his dancing **embarrassed** his **wife.**

(2 Samuel 6:16)

The
**prophet
Isaiah**
walked around **naked**
and **barefoot**
FOR THREE YEARS.
(Isaiah 20:2–3)

When **Jacob** camped for the night, he used a **stone** for a **pillow**.

THAT DOESN'T SOUND VERY COMFORTABLE!

(Genesis 28:11)

Eww! John the Baptist ate BUGS and HONEY.

HOW WOULD YOU LIKE TO EAT THAT EVERY DAY?

(Matthew 3:4)

Four of **Jesus's twelve disciples** made a living as **fishermen.** **Peter** went back to fishing after Jesus died, and at least once, he fished without **wearing clothes!**

(Matthew 4:18–22; John 21:7)

The **BENJAMITE ARMY** once had **26,000** men. The **700** men who were left-handed **never missed** when they aimed their slingshots!

(Judges 20:15–16)

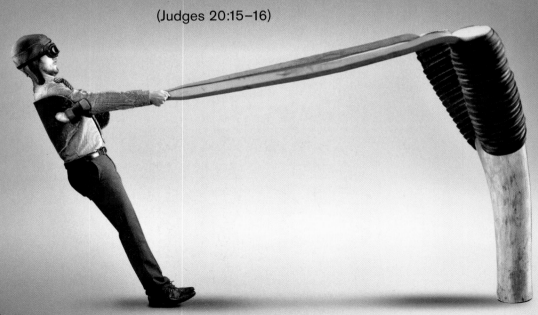

Sometimes it's okay to **LIE DOWN ON THE JOB!**
GOD instructed the **PROPHET EZEKIEL** to lie on his left side for **390** days and then turn over and lie on his right side for **40** days.

(Ezekiel 4:4–6)

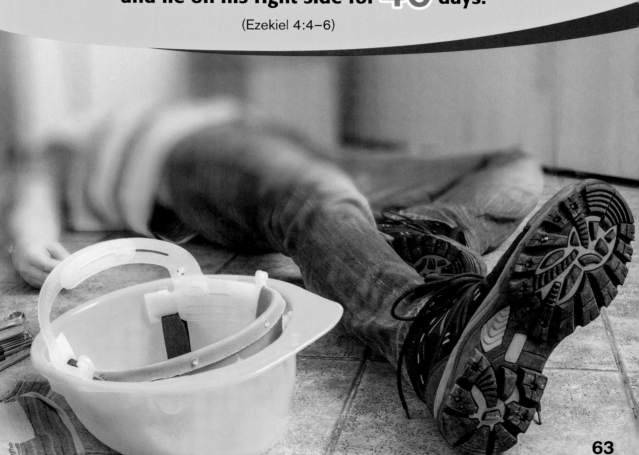

JOHN THE BAPTIST and **JESUS**
were related because their mothers,
ELIZABETH and MARY, were relatives.
Mary visited Elizabeth during Elizabeth's
sixth month of pregnancy.

(Luke 1:39–45)

According to **Genesis**, there was only one language until the **Tower** of **Babel.** Now there are about **7,000** languages in the world.

(Genesis 11:9)

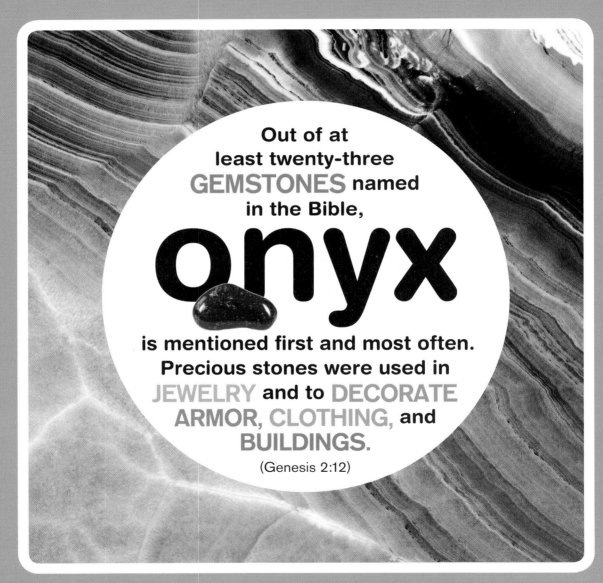

Out of at least twenty-three GEMSTONES named in the Bible,

onyx

is mentioned first and most often. Precious stones were used in JEWELRY and to DECORATE ARMOR, CLOTHING, and BUILDINGS.

(Genesis 2:12)

Proverbs says that **lazy people** should watch  **ants** and learn from them, because **ants** are very

HARD WORKERS.

(Proverbs 6:6)

Camels are a major form of transportation in the Bible. Camels have three eyelids on each eye. Two of the eyelids have **eyelashes** to keep sand out of their eyes. The third, which is **see-through,** works like a **windshield wiper,** allowing camels to see during a sandstorm.

(Isaiah 21:7)

REHOBOAM

had **88 CHILDREN,**
the same number as the keys on a piano.

(2 Chronicles 11:21)

The name of **GOD** is **NOT MENTIONED** in the book of **ESTHER.**

(Esther)

There are almost a **MILLION** species of insects known in the world today. Only 16 are mentioned by name in the Bible, but three of the ten plagues — **GNATS, FLIES,** and **LOCUSTS** — truly "bugged" the people of Egypt! (Exodus 8:17, 24; 10:13–14)

The Bible describes **GIANTS** who were
MIGHTY WARRIORS.
DAVID not only defeated a giant named
GOLIATH,
but he and his men also
KILLED
OTHER GIANTS
who warred
against Israel.

(2 Samuel 21:22;
1 Chronicles 20:6–8)

ACHOO! Salt

is referred to more than **two dozen times** in the Bible,

but pepper is not mentioned at all.

(Mark 9:50)

According to some English translations of the Bible,

King Jehu

once drove his chariot like a

maniac.

(2 Kings 9:20)

The **Bible** says that a

foolish

person who keeps acting foolishly is like a

dog that vomits

and then eats it.

(Proverbs 26:11)

STAY AWAKE IN CLASS!

A young man **fell asleep** when the
APOSTLE **PAUL** **WAS TEACHING,**
and he fell out of a third-floor window.

(Acts 20:9)

Surprise!

When a group of Israelites was **burying a man,** they saw a band of raiders coming—so they quickly tossed the body into the prophet **Elisha's tomb.** As soon as the dead body touched Elisha's bones, the man **came to life again!**

(2 Kings 13:20–21)

When some kids **MADE FUN** of the prophet Elisha's **BALD HEAD**, two **bears** attacked them.

(2 Kings 2:23–24)

King Eglon was

SO FAT

that when an attacker **stabbed** him, the entire sword— including the hilt— **disappeared** into the king's **belly.**

(Judges 3:21–22)

How could a **paralyzed** man get through a crowded house to see Jesus? His friends carried him there, CUT A HOLE IN THE ROOF, and then lowered him through the hole into the house.

(Mark 2:1–5)

JESUS gave thanks

for his food, such as when he fed about

4,000 people.

(Mark 8:1–9)

It's not polite to point!

When **King Jeroboam** STRETCHED OUT HIS HAND to God's prophet and yelled, **"Seize him!"** the hand he was pointing with suddenly **shriveled up.**

(1 Kings 13:4–5)

Methuselah,

the OLDEST man in the Bible, lived to be

969

years old.

THAT'S A LOT OF **BIRTHDAY CANDLES!**

(Genesis 5:27)

NUTS that are mentioned in the Bible include pistachios and almonds.

(Genesis 43:11)

King Solomon's

temple included a cast-metal tub that held about
 15,000 gallons of water.
(That's more water than in an average
home swimming pool!)

(1 Kings 7:23; 2 Chronicles 4:5)

The **WISE MEN** didn't visit 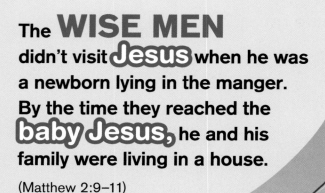 Jesus when he was a newborn lying in the manger. By the time they reached the **baby Jesus,** he and his family were living in a house.

(Matthew 2:9–11)

Although most animals came on

NOAH'S ARK in only one pair,

every type of **clean animal**

(the animals used for food and sacrifices)

came in

seven

pairs.

(Genesis 7:2–3)

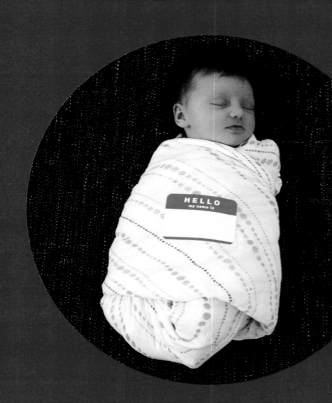

God named

five babies before they were born, including **John the Baptist. God took away** the **voice** of John's father until after HE WAS BORN!

(Genesis 16:11, 17:19;
1 Chronicles 22:9;
Matthew 1:21; Luke 1:13)

One king had couches of gold and silver.

(Esther 1:6)

YOU PROBABLY WOULDN'T LET YOUR DOG JUMP UP ON THOSE!

Elijah the prophet once ran faster than a chariot pulled by horses.

(1 Kings 18:46)

Jesus fed his disciples a **fish breakfast** after the **Resurrection.**

(John 21:9)

The Bible often calls people **sheep,** and both **God** and **Jesus** are referred to as **shepherds.**

(Psalm 100:3; John 10:14–15)

Ever wish you had more hours in a day? When **Joshua** was **fighting a battle,** he asked **GOD** to give him **more time—** so the sun stood still **for a full day!**

(Joshua 10:12–13)

Jesus wasn't always calm. The Bible tells us that he got angry and sad.

(Mark 3:5; John 11:35)

Samson, known for his **strength,** once killed **1,000** men with the **jawbone** of a donkey!

(Judges 15:15)

The **BIBLE** says a proud king spent

7 YEARS

living in the wild,

eating grass like an ox, and letting his fingernails grow long.

(Daniel 4:25, 33)

JESUS SLEPT each night like **you and I do.** One time he slept in the middle of a **BIG storm** even while his disciples were scared! (Luke 8:23)

The first time the Bible mentions a **man shaving**

is when **Joseph,** the son of **Jacob,** was in an **Egyptian jail** and **PHARAOH** wanted to see him.

(Genesis 41:14)

The **NOAH** who built the **ark** isn't the only Noah mentioned in the English Bible. Our **English Bibles** mention a **female Noah!** (Joshua 17:3)

Although
elephants and
hippopotami

are not mentioned in the Bible,

IVORY

—which is made from their tusks—is.

Ivory was valuable and was

USED AS MONEY

and to **decorate thrones.**

(Ezekiel 27:15)

The **COMMANDER** of an **army** was killed when a woman pounded a **tent peg** through his head.

(Judges 4:21)

There are three men in the Bible named

Dodo.

But the name doesn't refer to the extinct bird—the word *dodo* in Hebrew means **"his beloved"** or **"uncle."**

(Judges 10:1; 2 Samuel 23:9; 1 Chronicles 11:26)

Exodus 33:21–23
said **Moses**
wasn't allowed to see
God's face,
but he got to see
his back.

MOSES may have **stuttered** when he **spoke,** but **God** still showed Moses **how to lead.**

(Exodus 4:10)

God wrote the **TEN COMMANDMENTS** on stone tablets **twice.** Moses **broke the first set** when he saw the people **worshiping** a **CALF MADE OF GOLD.**

(Exodus 31:18, 32:19, 34:28)

105

The angel

Gabriel

brought messages to
several people in the Bible.

He explained a **vision** to
Daniel, **announced** to
Zechariah the birth of
John the Baptist,
and **told** **Mary** she would have a
son named Jesus.

(Daniel 8:16; Luke 1:13, 19, 26, 31)

Some **women** in the Bible **used makeup.**

(2 Kings 9:30; Esther 2:3,9)

In the Bible, some people claimed to **control animals** and **interpret dreams.**

(Exodus 8:7; Daniel 2:2)

The **prophet**
Elijah
didn't **die** but was taken
to heaven in a **fiery chariot**
PULLED BY HORSES OF FIRE.

(2 Kings 2:11)

109

PHOTO CREDITS

museum of the Bible

EXPERIENCE THE BOOK
THAT SHAPES HISTORY

Museum of the Bible is a 430,000-square-foot building located in the heart of Washington, D.C.—just steps from the National Mall and the U.S. Capitol. Displaying artifacts from several collections, the Museum explores the Bible's history, narrative, and impact through high-tech exhibits, immersive settings, and interactive experiences. Upon entering, you will pass through two massive, bronze gates resembling printing plates from Genesis 1. Beyond the gates, an incredible replica of an ancient artifact containing Psalm 19 hangs behind etched glass panels. Come be inspired by the imagination and innovation used to display thousands of years of biblical history.

Museum of the Bible aims to be the most technologically advanced museum in the world, starting with its unique Digital Guide that allows guests to personalize their museum experience with navigation, customized tours, supplemental visual and audio content, and more.

For more information and to plan your visit, go to
museumofthe**Bible**.org.